Table of Contents

It's a Party!........................... 4

Why Do We Have Political Parties?.... 6

Two-Party System 12

Third Parties..................... 24

What Do You Think? 28

    Glossary 30

    Read More.......................31

    Internet Sites 31

    Index 32

Glossary terms are **bold** on first use.

It's a Party!

You may have heard people talking about being members of a party. Maybe your dad is a member of the Democratic Party. Your mom is a **Republican**. Your grandpa said he's part of the Green Party. Say what? They're not talking about parties with balloons and cake. They belong to political parties.

The Republican and Democratic Parties are two political parties in the United States.

POLITICAL PARTIES

A Kid's Guide

by Cari Meister

CAPSTONE PRESS
a capstone imprint

Captivate is published by Capstone Press, an imprint of Capstone.
1710 Roe Crest Drive,
North Mankato, Minnesota 56003
www.capstonepub.com

Copyright © 2020 by Capstone. All rights reserved. No part of this publication may be reproduced in whole or in part, or stored in a retrieval system, or transmitted in any form or by any means, electronic, mechanical, photocopying, recording, or otherwise, without written permission of the publisher.

Library of Congress Cataloging-in-Publication data is available on the Library of Congress website.
ISBN 978-1-5435-9140-8 (library binding)
ISBN 978-1-4966-6604-8 (paperback)
ISBN 978-1-5435-9144-6 (eBook PDF)
Summary: Gives facts about political parties, their history, and how they play a part in U.S. elections.

Image Credits
Alamy: Jeffrey Isaac Greenberg 2, 10, Jim West, 29, Niday Picture Library, 26, Richard Ellis, 18, VWPics /Terray Sylvester, 11; AP Images: Chuck Burton, 22; Newscom: Everett Collection, 23 (Nast), Pacific Press/Andy Katz, 5 (top), Polaris/Phil McAuliffe, 27 (Stein and crowd), Reuters/John Hillery, 24, Reuters/Jonathan Ernst, 15, 27 (button), Roll Call Photos/Bill Clark, 28, UPI/Greg Whitesell, 17, UPI/Roger L. Wollenberg, 7, ZUMA Press/Erik Mcgregor, 14, ZUMA Press/Eve Edelheit, 8, ZUMA Press/US Senate, 9; Shutterstock: DNetromphotos, 12, Everett - Art, 5 (bottom), Jane Kelly, Cover, 1, Joseph Sohm, 25, mark reinstein, 20, Nerthuz, 16 (donkey), 23 (elephant), pathdoc, 4, Peeradach R, 6; U.S. Navy photo by Mass Communication Specialist 3rd Class Grant G. Grady, 21; Wikimedia/Bureau of Engraving and Printing/Restoration by Godot13, 16 (Jackson)

Design Elements
Capstone; Shutterstock: openeyed

Editorial Credits
Editor: Michelle Parkin; Designer: Bobbie Nuytten;
Media Researcher: Jo Miller; Production Specialist: Laura Manthe

All internet sites appearing in back matter were available and accurate when this book was sent to press.

A supporter of Bernie Sanders showed his platform.

A political party is a group of people who share the same ideas about how the U.S. government should run. Parties put these ideas into their party **platform**. You can't stand on this platform. It's a written document that lists the party's goals and beliefs.

FACT: George Washington was the only president who did not belong to a political party.

Why Do We Have Political Parties?

The goal of any political party is to be in charge of the U.S. government. They want to make laws and policies that support their platforms. How do they do this? Members of the party need to be elected to government positions to make decisions.

People vote for members of political parties.

Former president George W. Bush is a member of the Republican Party.

In the United States, people vote for our leaders. Voters pick the **candidates** they believe will do the best job. A candidate is someone who is running for office. Voters may choose a candidate who belongs to the same political party. They could also vote for the person who shares the same views about government.

7

Let's say a voter wants to pay fewer taxes each year. Another wants the government to spend more money on educational programs for kids. A third voter wants college to be less expensive. Another wants the government to spend more money exploring space.

Volunteers talked to a voter about their candidate for mayor.

Democratic senator Elizabeth Warren talked about student loan debt.

Political parties have very different views on these issues—and many others. Not everyone agrees. A voter looks for the political party and candidates that match his or her own views.

If you belong to a certain political party, you may think the party's candidate has the same views as you. That may not be true. Not all people in the same political party believe the same things. It's important for voters to research a candidate's opinions and platform before voting.

Voters should learn about what each candidate stands for before voting.

POLITICAL PARTIES AND THE ELECTION

During an **election**, candidates from different political parties run against each other. But before this happens, the political party needs to pick a candidate to represent them in the election. Members of the same political party meet at that party's national **convention**. The main goals of a national convention are to pick the party's candidates for president and vice president. They also decide on the party's platform.

Two-Party System

There are two main political parties in the U.S.—the Democratic Party and the Republican Party. These two parties run a lot of positions in our government. Because of this, our government is often said to be a two-party system. Let's find out how these parties formed and what they stand for.

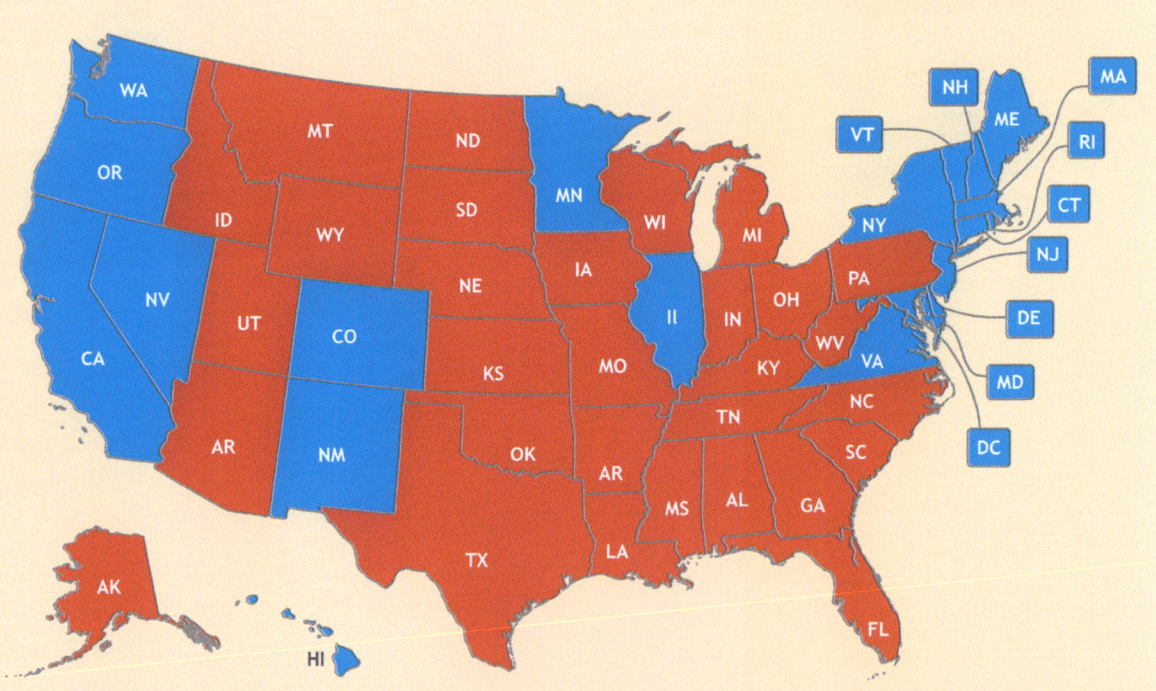

Democratic Party

The Democratic Party is the oldest political party around today. It was **founded** in 1828. That's more than 200 years ago!

The first Democratic president was Andrew Jackson. He was America's seventh president. He served from 1829 to 1837. There have been 15 Democratic presidents so far.

DEMOCRATIC PRESIDENTS

PRESIDENT	TIME IN OFFICE
Andrew Jackson	1828–1832
Martin Van Buren	1837–1841
James K. Polk	1845–1849
Franklin Pierce	1853–1857
James Buchanan	1857–1861
Andrew Johnson	1865–1869
Grover Cleveland	1885–1889 and 1893–1897
Woodrow Wilson	1913–1921
Franklin D. Roosevelt	1933–1945
Harry S. Truman	1945–1953
John F. Kennedy	1961–1963
Lyndon B. Johnson	1963–1969
Jimmy Carter	1977–1981
Bill Clinton	1993–2001
Barack Obama	2009–2017

The Democratic Party believes in a big government. The party supports large education and social programs. For example, they believe the government should pay for things like preschool. Many **Democrats** also want strict gun laws to protect **citizens**.

Congresswoman Yvette Clarke talked about gun violence and gun laws in the U.S.

The Democratic Party believes the government should pay for mental health programs. They also think everyone should have healthcare, even if they can't pay for it. The Democratic Party believes that wealthy people should pay for programs that help people who are poor.

Does this mean you have to agree with all of these platforms to be a Democrat? Of course not! You can still belong to a political party even if you disagree with some of the party's beliefs.

Democratic senator Nancy Pelosi talked about changing U.S. gun laws.

The Democratic Party and the Donkey

Have you seen the donkey **symbol** during elections? It represents the Democratic Party. It started way back in 1828. Democratic candidate Andrew Jackson was running for president. Another candidate called Jackson a donkey. Instead of getting mad, Jackson laughed. Donkeys are strong and smart. They can also be stubborn. Jackson liked being compared to the animal. He put an image of a donkey on his **campaign** posters.

Andrew Jackson

Jackson won the election and became U.S. president. Years later, cartoonist Thomas Nast used an image of a donkey to stand for the Democratic Party. The symbol stuck.

FACT: People who are democrats can also be called liberals and progressives.

A supporter wore a donkey hat to the Democratic National Convention in 2004.

Republican Party

The Republican Party hasn't been around quite as long as the Democratic Party. It was created in 1854. The first Republican candidate ran for president in 1856. His name was John C. Frémont. He lost.

The first Republican president was Abraham Lincoln. He was elected in 1860. So far, there have been 19 Republican presidents.

FACT: Ronald Reagan was the first Republican president to be a former member of the Democratic Party.

The Republican National Convention in Ohio.

FACT: The Republican Party is also called the GOP. This stands for Grand Old Party. This nickname has been around since the 1870s.

REPUBLICAN PRESIDENTS

PRESIDENT	TIME IN OFFICE
Abraham Lincoln	1861–1865
Ulysses S. Grant	1869–1877
Rutherford B. Hayes	1877–1881
James A. Garfield	1881
Chester A. Arthur	1881–1885
Benjamin Harrison	1889–1893
William McKinley	1897–1901
Theodore Roosevelt	1901–1909
William Howard Taft	1909–1913
Warren G. Harding	1921–1923
Calvin Coolidge	1923–1929
Herbert Hoover	1929–1933
Dwight D. Eisenhower	1953–1961
Richard Nixon	1969–1974
Gerald Ford	1974–1977
Ronald Reagan	1981–1989
George H.W. Bush	1989–1993
George W. Bush	2001–2009
Donald Trump	2016–

The Republican Party chose Donald Trump as their candidate in 2016.

Today, the Republican Party believes in a smaller government. This means they don't think the government should be involved in all parts of a person's life. They believe that big government gets in the way of a person's freedoms.

The Republican Party wants a strong military. This means they believe that the United States should do what is needed to protect itself from enemies around the world. This includes making sure there are enough weapons and equipment. It also means training people to fight against **terrorism.**

FACT: Republicans are also called conservatives.

A strong U.S. military includes Navy ships that help protect citizens.

What else is on the Republican Party's platform? They believe in lower taxes and less government spending. The party is also against a government-run healthcare system.

They think that parents should be able to choose where their children go to school and use their tax dollars for those schools. The party believes the harder that each person works, the stronger the country will be as a whole.

A woman talked about the upcoming Republican National Convention in 2020.

The Republican Party and the Elephant

The elephant symbol is used to represent the Republican Party. It all started with a cartoon in 1874. Thomas Nast drew an elephant for the Republican Party. Nast never explained why he used an elephant. However, some people believe that it was because an elephant is big and strong, just like the Republican Party.

Thomas Nast

Third Parties

Now you know some differences between the two major political parties. But what if you don't want to be a member of either party? Don't worry. There are other political parties in America. These are called third parties. A third party is any political party that is not Democratic or Republican. They may not have as many members, but they are important.

A speaker at the Reform Party National Convention in Dearborn, Michigan

Third party candidates can impact election results. For example, Independent candidate Ross Perot ran for president in 1992. Although he didn't win, Perot received almost 20 million votes. In 1998, Reform Party member Jesse Ventura won Minnesota's election for governor.

Independent Ross Perot ran for president in 1992.

Some third parties last only a few years. Others have been around for a long time. The Socialist Party has been around since 1901. Over the years, they have fought for things like better pay for workers.

A campaign poster for a Socialist Party candidate from 1901

FACT: The Federalist Party was one of the first political parties created in the United States. The party's last presidential candidate ran in 1816.

The Libertarian Party started in 1971. This party believes less government is better. They believe in freedom and **liberty** for each person. The Green Party started in the 1980s. They fight for clean air and water. They also want to use more land for national forests.

Green Party candidate Jill Stein spoke with supporters in Pennsylvania.

What Do You Think?

Are you ready to join a political party? This is an important decision. Think about each party's platform and what it means to you. Look online and research each candidate in the next election. Talk about issues that you care about with your friends and family. Make sure to look into what each party believes. Sometimes people's opinions online and on TV can make a party look like something it's not.

Student republicans from Florida State University met with former candidate Dale Peterson (center) in 2010.

Student volunteers made campaign signs.

When you've selected a political party, ask yourself if you can tell people your reasons why. If you are not sure, do some more research. When you are ready, go online and look for ways to help. You may be too young to vote for your favorite candidate. But you can help your political party in other ways. **Volunteer** to hand out flyers or help out at party meetings. Get involved. The future of politics depends on you!

Glossary

campaign (kam-PAYN)—organized actions and events with a specific goal, such as being elected

candidate (KAN-duh-dayt)—a person who runs for office

citizen (SI-tuh-zuhn)—a member of a country or state who has the right to live there

convention (kuhn-VEN-shuhn)—a large gathering of people who have the same interests

Democrat (DE-muh-krat)—a member of the Democratic party, one of two major political parties in the U.S.

election (i-LEK-shuhn)—the process of choosing someone or deciding something by voting

found (FOUND)—to set up or start something

liberty (LIB-ur-tee)—freedom from restriction or control

platform (PLAT-fohrm)—a statement of beliefs

Republican (ri-PUHB-lik-ahn)—belonging to the Republican party, one of two major political parties in the U.S.

symbol (SIM-buhl)—a design or object that stands for something else

terrorism (TER-ur-i-zuhm)—the use of threats or force to frighten or harm others

volunteer (vol-uhn-TIHR)—offer to work without pay

Read More

Bard, Mariel, and Jonathan Bard. *Republicans and Democrats.* New York: Power Kids Press, 2019.

Jeffries, Joyce. *What Are Political Parties?* New York: KidHaven Publishing, 2019.

Krasner, Barbara. *A Timeline of Presidential Elections.* North Mankato, MN: Capstone Press, 2016.

Internet Sites

PBS You Choose: Meet the President
https://pbskids.org/youchoose

Two-Party System
https://www.ducksters.com/history/us_government/two-party_system.php

Index

candidates, 7, 9, 10, 11, 16, 18, 28, 29

Democratic Party, 4, 12, 13, 14, 15, 16, 17, 18
Democrats, 15
donkeys, 16, 17

elections, 11, 17, 25, 28
elephants, 23

Green Party, 4, 27

Independents, 25

Libertarian Party, 27

Nast, Thomas, 17, 23
national conventions, 11

platforms, 5, 6, 10, 11, 15, 22, 28
presidents, 11, 13, 16, 17, 18

Reform Party, 25
Republican Party, 12, 18, 20, 21, 22, 23
Republicans, 4, 18, 24

Socialist Party, 26

two-party system, 12

voting, 7, 8, 9, 10